Feba Susan Thampi

# Proactive and reactive hierarchical routing protocols. A Survey

GRIN Publishing

**Bibliographic information published by the German National Library:**

The German National Library lists this publication in the National Bibliography; detailed bibliographic data are available on the Internet at http://dnb.dnb.de .

**Imprint:**

Copyright © 2014 GRIN Verlag GmbH
Print and binding: Books on Demand GmbH, Norderstedt Germany
ISBN: 978-3-656-59567-0

**This book at GRIN:**

http://www.grin.com/en/e-book/268519/proactive-and-reactive-hierarchical-routing-protocols-a-survey

**GRIN - Your knowledge has value**

Since its foundation in 1998, GRIN has specialized in publishing academic texts by students, college teachers and other academics as e-book and printed book. The website www.grin.com is an ideal platform for presenting term papers, final papers, scientific essays, dissertations and specialist books.

**Visit us on the internet:**

http://www.grin.com/

http://www.facebook.com/grincom

http://www.twitter.com/grin_com

# Proactive and reactive hierarchical routing protoc

# In wireless sensor networks-A Survey

Feba Susan Thampi, Department of Information Technology, Karunya University,Combatore-Tamilnadu

## Abstract

The application of wireless sensor networks a increasing day by day. As the demand for this network increase so is the need to evaluate the characteristics of the existing networks so as to maximize the performance of these networks. Once implemented, the network is in- accessible to the user hence the design of the network should be in an energy efficient manner. Wireless sensor networks are formed by a number of sensor nodes which are battery powered with limited energy available per node. Wireless sensors are not only used for monitoring but also for gathering data from the network. Extracting data should be performed with minimized energy as sensor networks are battery powered and wastage of which will result in the inefficient functioning of the network. The Low Energy Adaptive Clustering Hierarchy (LEACH) is the most popular protocol in this category which is based on adaptive clustering technique. This paper presents a study on the various cluster-based routing protocols and their performance in simple wireless network in terms of routing and energy issues related to it.

**Keywords**: Wireless Sensor Networks(WSN), Routing Protocols, energy efficiency, cluster head.

## I.INTRODUCTION

Wireless sensor networks consists of sensor nodes that are interconnected and they are controlled by a base station(BS).Routing protocol for wireless sensor networks is designed for two reasons: to increase the performance and efficiency of the network. Routing can be broadly classified into three categories based on the underlying network structure: flat, hierarchical, and location routing. In case of flat routing, all nodes are typically assigned equal roles or functionality. In hierarchical routing, nodes play different roles in the network. In case of location routing, sensor nodes' positions are exploited to route data in the network.

In case of adaptive routing, certain system parameters can be controlled in order to adapt to

In addition to the above, routing protocols can be subdivided into three categories, namely, proactive, reactive. And hybrid protocols depending on how the source node finds a route to the destination node. In case of proactive protocols, all the routes are calculated before they are really needed, while in reactive protocols, routes are calculated based on demand. Hybrid protocols use a combination of these two protocols. When sensor nodes are static, it is better to have table driven routing protocols rather than reactive protocols. A huge amount of energy is used in discovery of routes and setup of reactive protocols. Next class of routing protocols is called the cooperative routing protocols. In case cooperative routing, nodes send data to a central node where the data can be aggregated and can be subject to further processing if needed, hence reducing route cost in terms of energy use. Many other protocols rely on timing and position information.

## II.GENERAL CLASSIFICATION OF WIRELESS SENSOR NETWORKS - ROUTING CHALLENGES

Based on the mode of operation and the type of target application sensor networks can be classified [11] into two major types. They are:

### A. Proactive Networks
The nodes perform sensors-switching and transmitters sense the environment periodically and transmit the sensed data to a BS through the predetermined route. At regular intervals they provide a snapshot of the cluster and its sensed data. This type is suitable for applications that require periodic monitoring of data in network.

### B. Reactive Networks
The nodes in this network react immediately to sudden changes in the value of the sensed attribute beyond some pre-determined threshold value. They are therefore suited for time critical applications like military surveillance or temperature sensing.

*Challenges in Routing*

Routing in wireless sensor networks is very challenging due to several characteristics that distinguish them from contemporary communication and wireless ad hoc networks.

1. **Global Addressing Scheme**: It is impossible to build a global addressing scheme for the deployment of
Large number of sensor nodes. Hence, classical IP-based protocols cannot be applied to sensor networks.
2. **Flow of Data**: In contrast to typical communication networks almost all applications of sensor networks require the flow of sensed data from multiple
Sources to a particular sink.
3. **Redundancy in Data**: Generated data traffic has significant redundancy in it since multiple sensors may generate same data within the vicinity of a phenomenon. Such redundancy needs to be utilized by the routing protocols to improve energy and bandwidth utilization.
4. **Physical Constraints**: Sensor nodes are tightly constrained in terms of transmission power, on-board energy, processing capacity and storage and thus require careful resource management.

## III.ENERGY-EFFICIENT HIERARCHICAL ROUTING

This refers to the type of routing in wireless sensor networks in which the nodes are usually divided into several clusters, where each cluster consists of cluster heads and a number of cluster membership. A cluster head has the responsibility of routing from one cluster to the other cluster heads or base stations. Multiple cluster heads form the high-level network. With the advantages of convenient topology management, Hierarchical routing protocol has become the focus of the routing technology due to its high-efficiency energy use, and simple data fusion [1]. Data travel from a lower clustered layer to a higher one. Since it covers larger distances as it hops from one node to another, theoretically, the latency in such a model is much less than in the multihop model.

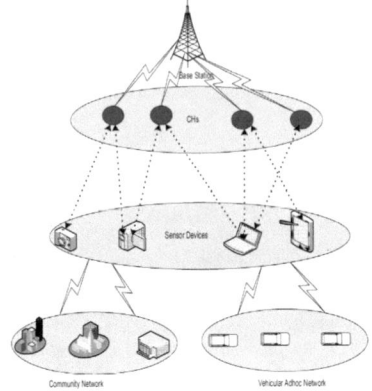

*Figure1: Generalised view of WSN*

### A. Proactive Network Protocols

### 2.1. Low-Energy Adaptive Clustering Hierarchy (LEACH)
LEACH [1][3] is the first hierarchical protocol of wireless sensor networks. LEACH has characteristics of low consumption and long survival of network. It is based on data fusion and plays an important role in routing protocol of wireless sensor networks. Other cluster-based routing protocols such as TEEN, APTEEN, and PEGASIS are evolved from the LEACH. The idea used here is to form clusters of the sensor nodes based on the received signal strength and local cluster heads are used as routers to the Base station (BS). Only the cluster heads will perform transmission hence energy can be saved as that compared to the scenario where all the nodes transmit. Optimal number of cluster heads is estimated to be 5% of the total number of nodes. Data processing such as data fusion and aggregation are local to the cluster. In order to balance the energy dissipation of nodes cluster heads change randomly over time. This decision is made by the node choosing a random number between 0 and 1 and this happens in a circular fashion .Each one round contains the set-up phase and steady phase. During the set-up phase, the cluster head is generated randomly, the random number is selected in a range between 0 and 1 in each sensor node, if the number selected is smaller than some threshold value say T (n), then that node is selected as the cluster head.

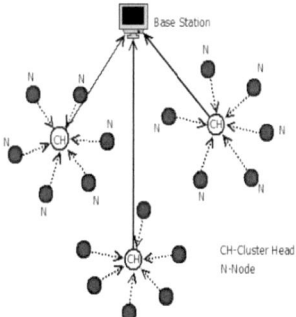

*Figure2: Clustering of Sensor Nodes*

The Formulae of T (n) is as follows:

$$T(n) = \begin{cases} \dfrac{P}{1-P*(r\,mod\frac{1}{P})} & \text{if } n \in G \\ 0 & \text{otherwise} \end{cases}$$

Where, p is the percentage of the total number of nodes in network including the cluster head, r is the present round number, G is the cluster node set except cluster head of the last 1/p rounds. Using this threshold value T (n), each node will be a cluster head at some point within 1/p rounds. A Node that was cluster head cannot become cluster head for a second time for
1/p -1 rounds. After that, in every round each node has a probability of 1/p of becoming a cluster head. At the end of every round, every normal node other than the cluster head selects the nearest cluster head and joins that cluster to transmit data. In this algorithm, the energy consumption will allocate approximately uniformly among all nodes and the non-head
nodes are turning off as much as possible. It also assumes that all nodes are in range of wireless transmission of the base station which is not the case in many sensor deployments. A node becomes broadcast to the entire network when it becomes the cluster head. Each node decides to join which cluster based on the strength of information received, and respond to the corresponding cluster head. In the next phase, each node uses the TDMA method to transmit data to the cluster head node; the cluster head will send the fusion data to the BS node. Each cluster completes communication channel with CDMA protocol between the clusters. Once the steady phase is over, the network enters the next round of the cycle again, and continuous cycle.

Advantages

a) Random selection of cluster head avoids excessive consumption of energy hence improves the network lifetime
b) Since LEACH [2] strategy is completely distributed, it reduces energy consumption 4 to 8 times lower in case where packets are relayed in multi-hop transmission.
c) LEACH [2][9] reduces 7 to 8 times low overall energy dissipation as compared to direct transmissions and minimum transmission energy routing.
d) In completely distributed network, sensor nodes do not require knowledge of global network.
e) All CH nodes die after the same time due to even head allocation.

Disadvantages

a) The protocol still uses the hop communication; hence nodes require a high power communications because each Cluster-Head directly communicates with BS, no matter the distance between CH and BS. Energy consumption will increase with distance.
b) b) Poor scalability hence not suitable for large-scale networks.
c) It does not provide clarity about position of sensor nodes and the number of cluster heads in the
d) Network.
e) Frequent selection of cluster head will lead to the traffic costing of energy.
f) The CH uses most of its energy for transmitting and collecting data, because, it will die faster than other nodes.
g) The CH is always on and when the CH die, the cluster will become useless because the data gathered by cluster nodes will not reach the base station.

2) *Centralized LEACH (LEACH-C)*
:

LEACH-C [2] is an enhancement of the LEACH protocol. A centralized clustering algorithm that is used i.e., it utilizes base station for cluster formation. It can produce better performance by spreading the cluster heads throughout the network. During the initial phase of LEACH-C,
Each node sends information about its current location and residual energy level to the base station. In addition to determining good clusters, the BS ensures that the energy load is evenly distributed among all the nodes. BS computes the average node energy, and determines which nodes

have energy below this average. The BS finds $k$ optimal clusters. Once the cluster heads and associated clusters are found, the BS broadcasts a message that obtains the cluster head ID for each node. If the ID of cluster head matches its own ID, then it is a cluster head; otherwise the node determines its TDMA slot for data transmission and

Goes to sleep until it's time to transmit data is reached. The steady-state phase of LEACH-C is similar to the LEACH protocol.

Advantages

a) The performance of LEACH-C is better than conventional LEACH because the BS utilizes global knowledge of the network to produce better clusters based on less energy for data transmission.
b) It also checks if the number of cluster heads in each round of LEACH-C equals a predetermined optimal value, whereas for LEACH the number of cluster heads varies from round to round due to the lack of global coordination among nodes.

### 3) SEP (Stable Election Protocol)

SEP[5][9]method is developed from LEACH which is based on the heterogeneity of networks. In This method, the high energy nodes are called as advanced nodes and their probability of becoming CHs is more as compared to that of normal nodes. SEP protocol is based on two levels of heterogeneity.

- let, $m$ is the fraction of the total number of nodes $n$, which is deployed with $a$ times more energy than the others. These powerful nodes are as advanced nodes,
- the number of normal nodes is $(1 - m) \times n$.
- ·Let the probability of normal nodes to become CHs be

$$P_{nor} = \frac{P_{opt}}{1 + m.\alpha}$$

Let the probability of advanced nodes to become CHs be

$$P_{adv} = \frac{P_{opt}.(1 + \alpha)}{1 + m.\alpha}$$

Where, Pop is the optimal probability of each node to become CH. The selection of CHs is done randomly on the basis of probability of each node.BS obtain the message from CH which in turn obtained the message from sensor nodes. By increasing $P_{adv}$ or m, system can be further

improved. SEP method results in better network life time and stable time period due to the two level of heterogeneity provided by normal nodes and sensor nodes.

Advantages

a) In SEP [5], the sensor nodes need not be aware of the overall energy at each selection round.

Disadvantages

a) The drawback of SEP [5] is the the CH selection is not dynamic, which results in the early death of sensor nodes that are far away from the powerful nodes.

### B. Reactive Network Protocols

#### 1) Threshold sensitive Energy Efficient sensor Network protocol (TEEN):

TEEN [7] is a hierarchical clustering protocol designed for reactive networks which groups sensors into clusters with each led by a CH, in order to detect sudden changes in the sensed data the nodes are divided twice for grouping. There two levels are the hard threshold, which is the minimum of data transmission and soft threshold that specify the variation in data. If the sensed data is exceeding the hard threshold the first time, nodes can send data to the CH, and set the data as current hard threshold and save sensed data. The nodes can send data only if the monitoring data is greater than the hard threshold and the absolute difference with the sensed data is not less than the soft threshold, and then the new data can be set as the current hard threshold. The protocol reduces the amount of data transfer by this method.

Advantages

a) TEEN is useful time critical sensing applications.
b) Sensing consumes less energy than transmission, hence less energy consumption than proactive networks.

Disadvantages

a) The main limitation of this scheme is that it is not well suited for applications where the data is needed on a regular basis.
b) Another possible problem is to ensure that there are no collisions in the cluster.

#### 2) Adaptive Threshold Sensitive Energy Efficient Sensor Network Protocol (APTEEN):

The (APTEEN)[3] [8] is an extension to TEEN and aims at both acquiring periodic data as well as reacting to time critical events. Its architecture is same as in TEEN. When clusters are formed by the base station, cluster heads broadcast their attributes, threshold values, and transmission schedule to all nodes. CHs also perform data aggregation in order to save energy. APTEEN supports three different query types: historical type which is used to analyze past data values; one-time type which is used to take a current view of the network; and persistent type which is used to monitor an event for a period of time.

Advantages

    a)  It guarantees lower energy dissipation and a larger number of live sensor nodes.
    b)  APTEEN is a hybrid protocol that is both proactive and reactive

Disadvantages

    a)  main drawbacks is the overhead and complexity of forming clusters in multiple levels
    b)  implementing threshold based functions and dealing with attribute-based naming of queries.

*3) UCEESEP (Unequal Clustering Energy Efficient Stable Election Protocol)*

UCEESEP [5][9] is based on unequal clustering unlike LEACH, SEP and TEEN as these are based on the equal sized clustering. This protocol has three levels of heterogeneity based on the different energy levels of the sensor nodes:
1) Advanced Nodes 2) Intermediate Nodes 3) Normal Nodes
Advance nodes are nodes having energy greater than other nodes. While Intermediate nodes are nodes having with some e energy greater than normal nodes and less than advance nodes, while normal nodes are the pending nodes.

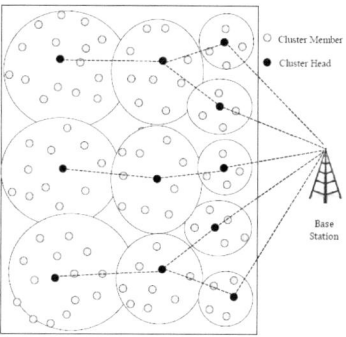

Cluster formation

UCEESEP is applicable where the time critical data reaches to the user almost instantaneously. Sensor nodes sense the data continuously but data packet transmission is not continuous as it consumes more energy as compared to sensing and processing. When the cluster head change take place, the threshold value is calculated with current and initial energy of the sensor node, so it is a better method for cluster head selection in UCEESEP protocol and most recent values of hard threshold, soft threshold, report time and attributes are transmitted, so user can predict the occurrence of sensed data values and application specific parameters. These attributes can be changed on the basis of requirement, as attributes are broadcasted at periodically.

Energy for normal nodes = $E$
Energy for advance nodes $E$adv $= E + \alpha$
Energy for intermediate nodes $E$int $= E (1 + \mu)$
Where, $\mu$
$\alpha$ factor for advanced nodes which has $\alpha$ times more
Energy than normal nodes.
Total energy of normal nodes $= n.b (1 + \alpha)$
Total energy of advance nodes $= nE (1\ bn)$
Total energy of intermediate nodes $= n. .E (1 + \alpha)$
Finally Total Energy of all the nodes $= nE .(1\ bn)$ $+n. .E .(1 + \alpha) + n.b.(1 + \mu) = n.E (1 + \alpha + b\mu)$
where,
$n$ = total number of nodes,
$m$ = proportion of advanced nodes,
$b$ = proportion of intermediate nodes,

Advantages

    a)  UCEESEP use unequal clustering, it balances the energy consumption among sensor nodes and enhances the network lifetime.
Disadvantage

    a) If threshold is not reached, the base station will not receive any information or data packets from sensor network.

## IV. CONCLUSION

Routing in sensor networks is an advancing research area, with limited but rapidly growing set of solutions. In this paper, hierarchial routing protocols are discussed based on two broad categories: Reactive and Proactive based on the type of application. selection of CH node is very important aspect and the major research going in the direction is focused on how to minimize energy consumption during the process of extracting the essential data as the SNs are powered by batteries which have limited energy. Clustering has been used widely for efficient routing for the data communication from SNs to BS. It has been observed in the literature that Clustering reduces the energy consumption which prolong the life time of WSN. Low Energy Adaptive Clustering Hierarchy (LEACH) protocol is the fundamen- tal clustering based routing protocol for WSNs. Taking LEACH as a benchmark protocol, various protocols have been developed. They have the common objective of trying to extend the lifetime of the sensor network Hierarchical routing maintains the energy consumption of sensor nodes and performs data aggregation which helps in decreasing the number of transmitted messages to base station. The concept of unequal clustering is used and cluster head selection is threshold as well as energy level based, due to three levels of heterogeneity and being reactive routing protocol, it produces increase in energy efficiency and enhanced network lifetime[10][4].

## REFERENCES

[1] 1.Mr. An kit Gupta, 2.Ms. Sangeeta Malik, 3.Ms. Monika Goyal, 4. Dr. Pankaj Gupta *Department Of CSE,* Vaish College of Engineering, Rohtak, " Clustering Approach for Enhancing Network Energy using LEACH Protocol in WSN" , International Journal of Wired and Wireless Communications Vol.2, Issue 1, October, 2012 , Print-ISSN: 2319-9512 e-ISSN: 2319-9520

[2] Dewey Xu, Jing Gao, "Comparison Study to Hierarchical Routing Protocols in Wireless Sensor Networks", 2011 3rd International Conference on Environmental Science and Information Application Technology (ESIAT 2011)

[3] Harneet Kour,"HIERARCHICAL ROUTING PROTOCOLS IN WIRELESS SENSOR NETWORKS", *International Journal of Information Technology and Knowledge Management,December 2012, Volume 6, No. 1, pp. 47-52*

[4] Dinesh Anand* & Sanjay Kumar,"HIERARCHICAL ROUTING PROTOCOLS IN WIRELESS SENSOR NETWORK", *International Journal of Information Technology and Knowledge Management January June 2009, Volume 2, No. 1, pp. 97-101*

[5] Sudhanshu Tyagia, Neeraj Kumar, Department of Electronics and Communication Engineering, JPIET, Meerut, UP, India, Department ofComputerScienceandEngineering,ThaparUniversity,Patiala,Punjab,India "A systematic review on clustering and routing techniques based upon LEACH protocol for wireless sensor networks" , Journal of Network and Computer Applications 36 (2013) 623–645

[6] Santosh Ahirwar , Pushpraj Tanwar ,*Electronics & Communication Engineering Department, Radharaman Institute of Technology & Science, Bhopal, India,*"Unequal Clustering Energy Efficient Stable Election Protocol in Wireless Sensor Network" ,International Journal of Emerging Technology and Advanced Engineering Website: www.ijetae.com (ISSN 2250-2459, ISO 9001:2008 Certified Journal, Volume 3, Issue 11, November 2013)

[7] Bara'a A. Attea∗, Enan A. Khalil ,Department of Computer Science, Baghdad University, Iraq ,"A new evolutionary based routing protocol for clusteredheterogeneous wireless sensor networks", Applied Soft Computing 12 (2012) 1950–1957.

[8] A. Manjeshwar and D. P. Agrawal," TEEN: A Routing Protocol for Enhanced Efficiency in Wireless Sensor Networks", *Int'l.Workshop on Parallel and Distrib. Computing Issues in Wireless Networks and Mobile Computing, April* 2001.

[9] Ningbo Wang, Hao Zhu, —An Energy Efficient Algorithm Based on LEACH Protocoll, International Conference on Computer Science and Electronics Engineering (ICCSEE), 2012, pp. 339-342.

[10] Ameer Ahmed Abbasi a,*, Mohamed Younis b, Department of Computing, Al-Hussan Institute of Management and Computer Science, Dammam 31411, Saudi Arabiab Department of Computer Science and Electrical Engineering, University of Maryland, Baltimore County, Baltimore, "A survey on clustering algorithms for wireless sensor networks" MD 21250, USA Available online 21 June 2007.